What is a Short Story?

Charlotte Guillain

raintree

a Capstone company — publishers for children

Raintree is an imprint of Capstone Global Library Limited, a company incorporated in England and Wales having its registered office at 7 Pilgrim Street, London, EC4V 6LB – Registered company number: 6695582

www.raintree.co.uk
myorders@raintree.co.uk

Edited by Clare Lewis and Holly Beaumont
Designed by Philippa Jenkins
Picture research by Wanda Winch
Originated by Capstone Global Library Ltd
Produced by Helen McCreath
Printed and Bound in China by CTPS

ISBN 978 1 406 29004 2
18 17 16 15 14
10 9 8 7 6 5 4 3 2 1

British Library Cataloguing in Publication Data
A full catalogue record for this book is available from the British Library.

Acknowledgements
We would like to thank the following for permission to reproduce photographs: Atinuke, artist, 20; Capstone Press: Karon Dubke, 26, 28; Corbis: Blue Lantern Studio, 25, Matthias Tunger, 27; Dreamstime: Diego Vito Cervo, 14, Rmarmion, 4; Getty Images Inc: Timelapse Library Ltd./Tony Evans, 17; iStockphoto: IndigoBetta, 15; Library of Congress: Prints and Photographs Division, 13, 18, 22; Newscom: Getty Images Inc: AFP/Peter Muhly, 21, Zuma Press/Geoff Swaine, 19; Shutterstock: andreiuc88, 10, Antonia Gravante, 8, Carla Castagno, 23, holbox, 11, KUCO, 24, Monkey Business Images, 5, Olga Popova, 16, PathDoc, 9, urfin, pencil, Vietrov Dmytro, 7, wavebreakmedia, 12.

Disclaimer
All the internet addresses (URLs) given in this book were valid at the time of going to press. However, due to the dynamic nature of the internet, some addresses may have changed, or sites may have changed or ceased to exist since publication. While the author and publishers regret any inconvenience this may cause readers, no responsibility for any such changes can be accepted by either the author or the publishers.

Contents

Some words are shown in bold, **like this**.
You can find out what they mean by
looking in the glossary.

Want to read something new?

Sometimes there is nothing better than to relax and take your time reading a great **novel**. At other times, you might want to read something quick that you can pick up again later, like a comic. If you like to read a complete story in one reading session, then a short story is perfect. While a novel is like a three-course meal, a short story is like a delicious snack.

What kind of books do you enjoy reading?

You might enjoy reading a story with friends and talking about it together.

Have you ever read any short stories? Perhaps the writers of some of your favourite novels have also written short stories. If you look in your library or local bookshop, you might see many collections of short stories on the shelves. If you've never read one, read on to find out more – you might discover something you really like!

See for yourself

Short stories are great for writing competitions because they don't take too long to write and the judges have time to read lots of entries. Search online for prize-winning short stories for children. What do you think makes these stories work?

What is a short story?

A short story is different to a **novel** or poem. It usually has the following features:

- A short story is **fiction** – the writer is telling the reader a story created by him or her, even if they got the idea from something that really happened.

- A short story is written in **prose**. This means it is not written in verse, like lots of poetry.

- Short stories are much shorter than novels. Often you can read a short story in one sitting, while a novel might take much longer. Short stories are not divided into chapters, but often focus on one or two moments or events.

See for yourself

Find a short story and look for the following:
- How many characters are there?
- Where does the story take place?
- How much time passes during the story?

Most short stories include just a few characters in one place for only a short length of time.

- A short story usually only has a few characters. The writer really focuses on these people and what is happening to them.

- Lots of short stories have a surprise twist at the end.

- Short stories often appear in a collection with other stories. Sometimes they are published in magazines.

Do you read any magazines that have short stories in them?

Characters

While a **novel** can have many characters with very different experiences and outlooks, a short story focuses in more closely on one or only a few characters. During the story, we learn about this character's personality and their actions in a short space of time, unlike in a novel where we can read about a character over many years. This means that when we read about characters in a short story, we are really zooming in on a part of their life and personality and exploring it in depth.

You get to know a character very quickly in a short story.

A short story writer can't spend too much time describing their characters or there would be no time left to tell the story! Good writers make sure they show the reader things, rather than just telling them. For example, they might describe a character's actions, and from the way they behave, we can learn what they are like.

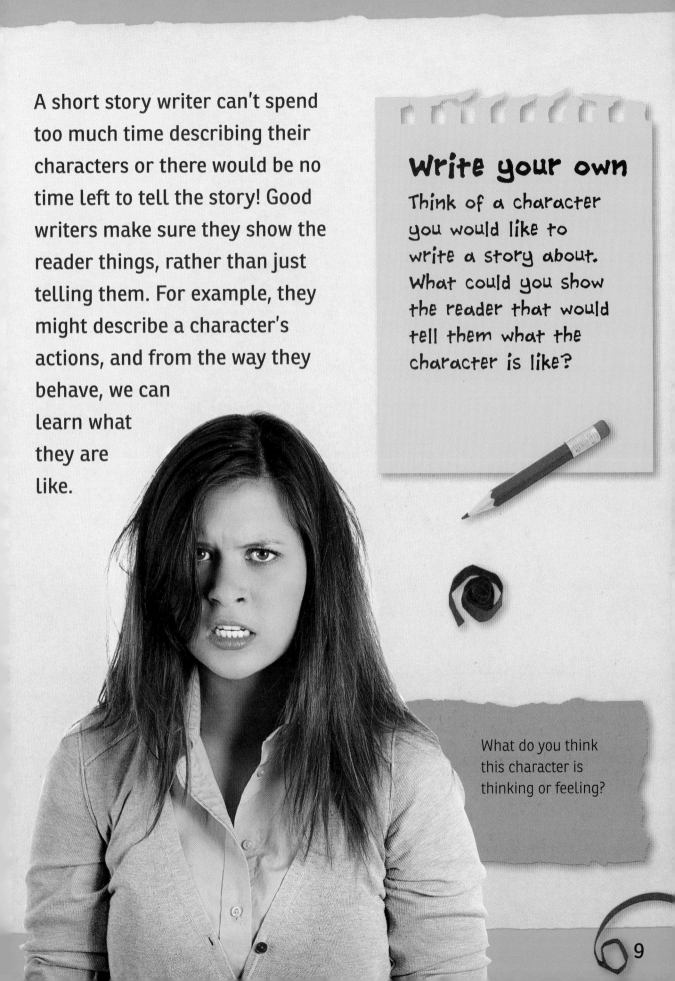

Write your own

Think of a character you would like to write a story about. What could you show the reader that would tell them what the character is like?

What do you think this character is thinking or feeling?

Setting

When starting to create a new short story, a writer thinks about the **setting**. This is where the events of the story take place, and could be a house, a city street or inside a spaceship. The setting also includes the time, season and weather.

In a short story the setting is important because it sets the mood. A strong setting builds atmosphere and helps to keep the reader hooked.

What sort of story might have a setting like this?

How would you describe the sights, sounds and smells of a setting like this?

Short story writers often use all of the senses to describe a setting. They think about what it looks like, the sounds and smells that the characters are experiencing, and even how things taste and feel. Using all of the senses makes sure the reader can imagine the setting very clearly. This means the writer can get on with telling the story.

Write your own

Close your eyes and think about the place where you want to set your story. What can you see and hear? Are there any smells around you? Are you hot or cold? Ask yourself lots of questions before you start to write.

First person or third person?

Short story writers have to decide whether to write in the **first person** or **third person**. Stories in the first person are told from the main character's perspective. This person narrates the story and talks about "I". For example, "I waded across the flooded street". The main advantage of writing in the first person is that the reader feels close to the narrator. This means they can really get under the skin of the main character and get to know them well.

Sometimes writers try out first and third person before deciding which to use in their story.

Charles Dickens also wrote novels in the first and third person.

Famous fiction

Charles Dickens (1812–1870) was a writer who wrote both long **novels** and short stories. *The Long Voyage* is a short story told in the first person by a character that loves to read about exciting adventures, but has never been anywhere himself. Because this story is short, using the first person allows Dickens to show us a lot about this main character and how he feels.

Other stories are written in the third person. This is when the writer steps back and describes what is happening to the characters from the writer's or narrator's viewpoint. For example, "Jenny waded across the flooded street". With the third person, the writer is able to tell us about what more than one character is thinking.

Plot

The **plot** is what happens in the story. When writers plan their stories out, they often begin with the plot. They work out what events will take place and in what order. It's important that the plot makes complete sense and has no loose ends.

The plot of a story must be original to keep the reader interested.

A story with a gripping plot will be hard to put down.

Usually what the main character in the story wants affects what happens in the plot. In a short story there will only be one or a few events, with a problem that the main character will have to overcome. There is often a surprise or twist at the end that the reader didn't see coming! In a short story everything that happens in the plot needs to be included for a reason. There is no room for extra details that are not important, or for **sub-plots**.

Write your own

When you are trying to come up with a plot for a short story, start with your main character. What do they want more than anything? What could be standing in his or her way? How will they deal with this problem? Finally, think of an ending that will surprise your readers.

Spooky and mysterious stories

Many well-known short stories are spooky or mysterious. Some of the most famous ghost stories and detective stories are short stories. A British writer called Sir Arthur Conan Doyle wrote short stories about the detective Sherlock Holmes. In each tale, Holmes solves a crime or mystery with his sidekick Dr Watson, often facing danger along the way. The American writer Edgar Allan Poe was well known for his scary short stories. Many of these are full of haunted houses and unexplained deaths.

Sherlock Holmes is one of the most famous fictional detectives in the world.

Famous fiction

You may have read some of Roald Dahl's children's books, such as *Charlie and the Chocolate Factory* and *Matilda*. He also wrote very scary short stories for grown-ups! Many of these have a dark sense of humour and they often have shocking **plot** twists. Some of Dahl's short stories were filmed for television.

Many of Roald Dahl's stories have dark and shocking characters.

Many of these **narratives** are told as short stories because this allowed the writer to keep up the tension. It would be much harder to keep the reader in **suspense** in a longer **novel**. Also, lots of these stories were first published in magazines, so they had to be quite short!

Funny short stories

A short story is a good way to tell a funny tale because the writer can focus on a central joke and build up a hilarious situation around a single moment or short sequence of events. The twist at the end of a short story can work in the same way as the **punchline** of a joke.

Mark Twain was well known for his sense of humour.

Famous fiction

Author Francesca Simon created the children's book character Horrid Henry. He appears in books made up of several short stories. Each one takes Henry through a funny situation. Even though he is rather horrible, the reader wants Henry to succeed – but he usually gets his comeuppance in the end.

Horrid Henry is a favourite funny children's book character.

Mark Twain was an American writer who wrote witty short stories as well as longer **novels**, such as *The Adventures of Tom Sawyer*. His short stories were published in newspapers and magazines. He also read them out loud to audiences around the United States. The short story suited these events perfectly because he could read a complete story to the people listening. Many of Twain's funny short stories were based on **observations** he had made in his own life about how people could be vain, foolish or misunderstand each other.

Short stories about real life

A lot of short story writers choose to describe real-life situations in their stories. They show us realistic moments in their characters' lives that might be very fleeting. Despite being only a small glimpse, the events in a good short story will stay in the reader's mind for a long time. When short stories are about real-life situations, the **settings** and characters are often very vivid and can feel real to the reader.

Atinuke's stories show us what real life is like in many parts of Africa.

Famous fiction

The Canadian writer Alice Munro is one of the world's most famous authors of short stories. She writes about people living in small towns who are facing problems in their apparently ordinary lives, and the situations she describes often leave the reader thinking about what they have just witnessed.

Alice Munro has won many prizes for her writing.

There are many short stories for children about people's "ordinary" lives. These include the *Anna Hibiscus* books written by Atinuke. These stories, about a girl growing up with her **extended family** in a busy African city, pick up on problems and experiences that all children are familiar with.

Fairy tales

Some of the first stories we ever hear are short stories. Fairy tales have been told and retold to children for centuries, and are perfect examples of short stories.

Famous fiction

Some of Hans Christian Andersen's most famous stories are *The Princess and the Pea*, *The Little Mermaid* and *The Emperor's New Clothes*. His stories often show readers that appearances are only skin-deep and that it's not right to judge people on what they look like or how wealthy they are.

Hans Christian Andersen (1805–1875) was a Danish writer who created many fairy tales.

The Brothers Grimm began writing down the folk tales they heard when they were growing up in Germany. Jacob (1785–1863) and Wilhelm (1786–1859) Grimm collected fairy stories and folk tales, such as *Cinderella, Hansel and Gretel* and *Snow White*. They wanted to discover and share the stories enjoyed by ordinary German people. Because these stories were originally told from memory, there were often different versions of them. The Brothers Grimm helped to create the version of each story that we know today.

The Brothers Grimm told one version of the *Little Red Riding Hood* story.

Myths and fables

The oldest short stories ever told or written down were probably **myths** and **fables**. Myths are very old, traditional stories that are often about ancient gods and heroes. For example, Greek myths are the stories and ideas of the ancient Greeks.

The ancient Greeks believed the stories told in their myths to be true. They described powerful gods and goddesses and the actions of brave heroes and heroines. The most famous myths include the story of Icarus, who flew too close to the Sun, and King Midas, who wished that everything he touched would turn to gold.

Icarus's wings were made out of feathers and wax by his father, Daedalus.

Fables are stories with a moral or lesson at the end. These stories are often short and involve just a few characters, usually animals. Some well-known fables are *The Hare and the Tortoise* and *The Lion and the Mouse*.

Write your own

Try writing your own fable. It's easiest to start with a moral, such as "appearances can be deceiving", "don't trust people who flatter you", or "the biggest isn't always the best". Try to build a story that shows this moral, with animals as your characters.

Finding the right short story for you

You have to hunt for short stories a bit more than other types of story. Often they are put in collections with other stories by different authors. This means you might discover new writers as you make your way through a collection. These books are also great to dip in and out of, because you don't have to follow a long **narrative** over time as you do with a **novel**.

Discover new authors as you explore short story collections.

There are so many short stories to enjoy when you know where to look for them.

It's a good idea to ask a librarian or bookseller for advice on finding different collections of short stories. If you want funny or spooky stories, they might be able to suggest suitable collections. Or, if you particularly like an author's style, they might be able to suggest a collection of their short stories.

Another place to find short stories is in magazines and comics. You could read them aloud with your friends and family and then talk about them afterwards.

See for yourself

Visit a website that sells books and search for "short stories for children". Have a look through the story collections that come up and see if you like the look of any of them. If you do, you could borrow the book from your library, or even buy a copy.

Take it further...

If you want to write a short story:

1. Always carry a notebook and pen so you can jot down ideas. This could be when you're on the school bus or walking around the supermarket!

2. Think carefully about the main character in your story. What does he or she want more than anything? How can you describe your character so that the reader knows as much as possible about his or her personality?

3. Spend time thinking about where and when your story is taking place. Close your eyes and ask yourself questions about the **setting**. Try to describe it so it appeals to all of the reader's senses.

4. Keep your **plot** simple and clear, with no unexplained events that are not important to the story. And try to come up with a sneaky twist at the end!

Ideas to get you started

A child is visiting his or her grandparents and is bored. He or she picks some books off the bookshelf and an old photo falls out of one book. Who is in the photo?

Your main character has got into trouble at school. They have just arrived home and found their mother on the phone to the head teacher. What do they do?

Your main character is hiking through the woods on a school trip. But he or she is separated from the group and gets lost. It's starting to get dark...

Glossary

extended family other members of your family apart from your parents and siblings; for example, grandparents, aunts, uncles and cousins

fable story with a moral

fiction story that has been made up

first person when the narrator of a story talks about "I" or "we"

myth very old, traditional story that is often about gods and the creation of the world

narrative account of events in a story

novel long story

observation something that the writer has noticed

plot storyline

prose writing that is not poetry

punchline final (and funniest) line of a joke

setting place and time that a story takes place

sub-plot less important strand of the story that happens alongside the main plot

suspense feeling of waiting for something exciting or scary to happen

third person when the narrator of a story talks about "her", "him" or "they"

Find out more

Books

Get Writing!, Paul Johnson (A&C Black, 2008)

How to Write Stories, Celia Warren (QED, 2008)

Write Your Own Story Book, Louie Stowell (Usborne, 2011)

Websites

www.theguardian.com/childrens-books-site
Read other children's recommendations for stories on this brilliant website, all about books.

www.booktrust.org.uk/books/children
The Book Trust website is great for helping you find stories across all different genres.

www.lovereading4kids.co.uk
Search for more recommended collections of short stories.

www.timeforkids.com/homework-helper/writing-tips
There are some excellent writing tips on this website.

Index